ye wee Scots laddie
wash yer oakies
ch luck

Gi

Back My SPERM

THOMAS

P.C.

CRAVEN

Millstone Visuals: http://www.tattiesoup.clara.net/

E-mail: ali@tattiesoup.clara.co.uk

DEDICATIONS

This book is dedicated to the memory of my father, George Craven, who died on the 10th of August 1989. Also to James Carr and James Argue, who are sadly missed, and to big Sanny Wingate, who is probably at this moment still arguing with God about some 'Old Firm' result from years ago.

ACKNOWLEDGEMENTS

I would like to thank the sponsors who helped me to get off the ground with my first book, 'Scotlands Own Campsie Characters'. Thanks to all my family and friends who gave me great encouragement. Also to Philip Differ who gave me the idea and to Bobby and Deirdre Forrest who came up with the idea for the front cover. Thanks again.

NOTE

There is no malice or ill intent in these few lines. I certainly, at my age, did not realise the consequences of having sexual relations. I do now. Also, the absolute stupidity of bigotry; it's time that this was put to sleep.

This is the hand that wrote it,

And therefore shall suffer first punishment.

Thomas Cranmer, 1489 - 1556

(at the stake)

O what a tangled web we weave,

When first we practice to deceive.

Sir Walter Scott, 1771 - 1832

Also by Thomas Craven and available at all good bookshops:

Scotlands Own Campsie Characters

Featuring:

The Hole In The Wall Gang and A Fish Called Kilmarnock

Text and Graphics by Ali Tait

CONTENTS

GIVE ME BACK MY SPERM

By

THOMAS P.C. CRAVEN

STARTING LINE

03:00 Hours. November 29th 1997

I love her, I love her not, I hate her, I hate her not. I want the baby, I want it not. I love roses, I hate them not. I love Celtic, I love them not. I hate Rangers, I hate them not. Och this is crazy.

My head is upside down, my feelings are in turmoil. What a situation I've got myself into. Forty-seven years of age and I'm going to be a dad, God help me.

I've been caught in the last furlong of spermhood. Stewards enquiry! Well I'm going to tell this story the way it happened, or should I say this race, this human race. This nine furlong race of fatherhood and motherhood.

So the story must go back to Boxing Day 1996. It's a bad time, or should I say a good time of year for me. My birthday is on the 27th of December, and as I love the horses, the beer and the women, not particularly in that order. Well you can imagine my sore head on the 28th. That's when I first really talked to Yvonne. She stayed two doors away from me.

Handy, eh! Handy my arse! Too handy as it turned out. She invited me in for a drink after the bells on Hogmanay, but I did not go, Id had enough at Xmas time. :Then little did I know that my card was marked. Oh yes well marked, by a very dubious tipster indeed. Well the money was down, the bet of life was struck.

But the real human race would not start till about July '97, when Yvonne would tell me she was pregnant. 'Allebloodylujah', I thought.

I did not know whether to laugh or cry.

She had told me she was on the pill, but the deed was done, and we would have to live with it. My first reaction was outrage. I did not want her to get pregnant. Or did I?

I am a typical Capricorn, I cannae help that. I am twenty years older than her and a year older than her mother, for Gods sake. One of the first things I thought of was an old 'Goldwynism' of Sam Goldwyns when he said, 'If I could drop dead just now, I would be the happiest man alive.'

Well the big handicap had started, the blinkers were on and I was heading straight for a brick wall. The brick wall of daddyhood. She had me tied hand and feet and nailed to the ceiling. Somebody help me. Then suddenly I remembered an old school pal of mine called Joe Gallagher, from Banknock. Joe got married at 16 years of age. That was about 1965. Obviously there was a shotgun involved. The next thing I heard, Joe had two or three weans. Then later on I heard he was split from his family.

What a shame, obviously he got married too young. It must have been devastating on the whole family. I often wonder where Joe is now. Maybe he done his 'McGill, Man In a Suitcase', or his 'Ben Gazzara, Run For Your Life', or maybe he headed for the beach or the tall trees, or parts unknown. Maybe he met Lord Lucan and they saddled up and rode into the sunset. I must digress at this point.

My uncle Charlie Leonard who also got married quite young, split up from his wife and headed for the California beaches. Well that didnae last long. Six months later he was back at home in Niagara Falls. He went to sign on at the local job centre, where they asked him what Indian reservation he was from. Charlie looked like a big Indian but obviously with the Scots accent, the tan and the big nose, they were a bit confused.

I'm glad to say Charlie and June got back together again. Lovely, eh?

Some guys can handle marriage and some can't. Not me.

So beware of the beautiful cunning fillies out there. When they are after you, you have no chance. They will tie you up like a turkey, then slowly cook you, and that my friends, will be your Coup de Grace.

THE FIRST FURLONG

About June7th – July 7th 1997.

Everything was going great, up 'till about April '97. I said to Yvonne, 'You will need to go on the Pill because I don't want you to get pregnant.' and she agreed. But little did I know that she had different plans. Stoap the race!

We had been seeing each other a couple of times a week, on very mutual terms. There was not any love between us, but maybe on her part. I suppose it was just a physical need after a few drinks but I remember what 'Roberto Burns' said; 'When guid drink goes in, guid sense goes out'.

Little did I know then, it wasn't the filly who was doped, it was the jockey. So there I was, cruising in the first furlong, but I was wearing the blinkers, not her. Maybe I should have worn something else. I must digress.

W.C Fields, who was a well-known horseplayer, once said, 'I was passing the racetrack one day, and it was closed, so I just threw my money under the gate'. Think about it, gambling, you have no chance. It's the same with women, you have no chance. Yvonne is a nurse, think about that. W.C Fields also said, 'Two days I was in the hospital and took a turn for the nurse'.

Well I should have took a turn, turned and ran. But I didnae. Like a mug punter, I kept on riding, riding on the losing bet. Stoap the race! So we were cruising up to the second furlong. Things were going great, Ha-bloody-Ha.

Yvonne was always putting notes through my door, wanting to see me, but mostly I just ignored them. The same feeling was just not there. It's not a very nice feeling, when someone has a lot of feelings for you, and you cannot return them. I know because it has happened to me.

When I was fifteen, I fell in love with a girl from Croy, but she fancied somebody else, and it really hurt me. Then when I was nineteen I fell in love with a girl from Kirkcaldy, same again. Maybe that's why I never got married, or I just did not meet the right girl. Those two encounters certainly made me very wary of women, and possibly a wee bit harder towards them.

But the end of the first furlong was getting closer, and I was about to get the latest news. Stoap the race!

The night Yvonne told me she was late, it did not really sink in. I asked her why. How is it possible? She said something about the doctor telling her to take the pill next week, or something. But as it turned out, it was pure fabrication. She wanted to get pregnant, and that was that. Maybe I would have felt different if she'd asked me. But no, she didnae. She had just backed a binger. I think it's a terrible thing to do, to anyone. That is, to take their feelings for granted. She obviously thought getting pregnant would change my feelings towards her. But it didnae. The emotional blackmail had started, and I did not like it, one bit.

I know when she reads this she will be angry, but it's the truth, every word. I'll show my arse at the top of the toon if I'm telling a lie.

Well, I had to talk to someone about it. I told my sister Tricia about it, and she said, 'Tam, maybe it's the best thing that's ever happened to you.' and maybe she was right. But I could not handle it, one second the going was good, then it was heavy. Then I told my Mother, and she said, 'I don't even know the lassie.'

I said, 'Ma, neither do I.'

Well, I had to go for a wee daunder. I managed to sprockle up the brae to sit at the 17th tee at Campsie Golf Club. It's a smashing view. You are sitting at the bottom of the Campsie Fells. Somedays it seems as though you can reach out and touch the Three Steps. Then you look up towards Campsie Glen, then away towards the Dumbarton Hills and Stockiemuir. The old memory starts reminiscing. Across the valley sits Lennox Castle and the hospital. For how long eh? Then I look down at St Machans School and the Bowling Club, and next to them is 'Boot Hill', which will be everyone's last furlong. What a strange and beautiful life this is. I shake my head back to the present moment. The race is moving on and Im feeling well within myself, as John

Francome says.

That was a long furlong, and there's still eight to go. So I'm gonnae go down to the Commancero, (Commercial), for a wee pint of black beer. Well, this racing makes you thirsty. The second furlong will come soon enough.

Frankie Dettori's seven winners at Ascot, must be the most amazing feat ever accomplished in the history of racing. What a man, one of the greatest jockeys that ever sat on a horse. Well, that day at Ascot, in the seventh race, Frankie was riding a horse called 'Fujiyama Crest!' A horse that could not win, according to the form anyway. But we all know about form, don't we?

Personally I think, if Frankie had been put on a three-legged, blind, wooden horse, he would still have won that race, because, it was written in the stars. It was meant to be. It's the same for me and you and everybody else and there's nothing we can do about it. Its kismet brother punters, and that's a fact, Jack.

CAMPSIE MAN TANNOCHSIDE

No place on Earth I'd rather be,
Than my dear home in Old Campsie,
Where as a boy I spent my days
On the Glaizert Banks and Sunny Braes,
Or up the line and Campsie Glen,
Beneath the towering Muckle Ben.
The Red Tub Tea Rooms to feed the hikers.
The Red Hills too where lived the Tinkers.
The fresh winds softly filled the air,
Oh happy then without a care.
Where characters were bred galore,
Rob Roy and young Jimmy Foyer.
And local worthies with awe the gen,
Tosh and Rod, Neilly the Yoke,
Proudly known as Campsie folk.
The football stars were there as well,
Some famous names one could tell.
The Lawsons, McLaughlans to name a few,
Big Geordie Thomson. Jock Britton too.
The pubs were plentiful to see
John Trowers across the road from me.
The Old Well Close and Lockarts Loan
Nae fridges, cars nor telephones.
But happy folk though poor they were,
A friendly neighbour on every stair.
Nae bigotry tae boot, in sight
Except pub rows and then a fight.
The Calico print works shed its dye
Into the burn, bright as sky.
And all the gifts bestowed their way
On my dear home in Old Campsie.
So when my time on earth is done,
Beneath the Hills that shade the sun,
Just lay me there to sleep and rest
Amongst the folks I've aye loved best.

John 'Tosh' McLaughlin of Clyde F.C.

Andrew 'Sanny' Wingate, goalkeeper, played in a charity game for Morecome.
Note Sir Stanley Mathews, back row second from the right

THE SECOND FURLONG

Approximately July 8th – August 8th

I was sitting in my flat one night talking to Yvonne about her being pregnant. I said to her, 'You planned all this, didn't you?' She thought for a couple of moments. Then I said, 'O.K. I want the truth'

'Yes I did.' She said.

'Why?'

'I planned it nine years ago, well I fancied you nine years ago. You used to go to the 'Posh Parrot' with your brother Michael, It was then that I fancied you. Then you moved in two doors away and I knew I had you hooked.'

I was stunned.

'So it was a trap then?'

'Well I suppose so.' She said.

So that was that, eh, after thirty-two years of freedom I had finally been snared. Somebody phone the polis. Nice one, eh?

But I did not like it, it made me angrier, and that feeling of being trapped was horrible. I asked her if she had told her family that she was pregnant.

'No.' She said.

'Well,' I said. 'Its about time you did.'

And so we fell out again. I did not realise what a tangled web I had got myself into. Stoap the race! So I headed for the 17th tee again, the next morning.

It was raining and the mist was halfway down the Campsie Fells but I didn't care, the weather summed up my feelings. As I sat there I thought about my predicament, and also about her angle, and what her game was. Well, obviously she was wanting a child and I was the red hot favourite, the job jockey the chosen sire. Often the odds-on-shots tend to get beat as we all know. She had anticipated my feelings, and you don't do that to anyone.

She had looked at me and seen, a forty-seven year old bachelor, who was vulnerable, a used to be stallion, who would be easy meat. A down and out punter, clutching at the straws of desperatism, who would relish being a father. Well she was wrang. She had seen me taking my sisters kids for wee walks, and thought, 'Oh he really likes kids.' W.C. Fields was once asked if he liked children, and he said, 'It depends which way they're cooked.' Well I had a similar feeling. I really do love children, but only for a wee while. After about two hours I've had enough. The anger was starting to leave me now. And the Capricorn part of my brain was taking charge.

I started to think maybe it would be nice living with Yvonne and the wean, and being a dad. Changing dirty nappies, up at all hours of the night, listening to a greetin wean. That'll be the day, nae chance. I was soon going to be forty eight years old, it was too late. Or was it? Take me drunk, I'm hame.

But you never know, maybe I would like it. We'll see, time will tell. But the going in this human race keeps changing. One minute I'm happy, then I'm sad, then I'm angry. What the hell is going on?

Talking about anger. I remember when Lester Piggott held up 'Sir Ivor' for a short devastating burst to win the Washington International in 1968. The American racing writers hammered him as a bum that nearly got the great horse beat. Then when Lester went back the following year and won the International again on 'Karabas', they suspected there might be more to him, and came crowding around with their questions. 'When did you think you had the race won, Lester - coming into the stretch, or a bit earlier?'

Lester's memory was as good as his riding. 'I thought I had it won three weeks ago.' He said, 'Now F— Off!'

Those guys should have known better than to mess with old stone face.

I was sitting there at the 17th tee, the sun was beginning to get through and the mist was rising. I was staring over at the graveyard, trying to pinpoint my father's grave. I wondered what old Geordie would have said if he knew I was going to be a dad. I can only guess, probably he would have said, 'Well ye'll hiv tae git merried Tam.'

No way Jose!

Then my mind started to race back to when father died: August the tenth 1989. And to a few months before, when I had won £15,000 on the horses; when my mother told me my father had cancer. Stoap the race!

The bet I put on was a double and two singles. The first horse was called 'Pilot', the mount of Willie Carson, £500 win. The other horse was called 'Reprimand', the mount of Stevie Cauthen, a £1000 win, and £500 double. Tax £200. Crazee Mental, eh? Well the whole world is Crazee Mental. But I took the chance, and it came off. 'Pilot' won at 11-4, and 'Reprimand', if my memory serves me right, opened at 5-2 and went out to 9-2, but cruised home easily with the six million dollar kid looking round two furlongs from home.

I was over zee moon. Nebuchadnazzer here I come! Obviously I gave some of my family and friends a few quid. It was then that I discovered I had more friends than I thought I had.

Derek Hendrie, who was with me when I won the money said when I put the bet on, 'Tam, yir aff yir heid.' He changed his opinion after the bet came up. I remember about a week later, when I finally came down off the clouds. I walked into my mother's house and handed Ma and Da two open return tickets to Toronto. My da was thrilled to bits. It's funny though, when you can detect that theres something wrong. I could see it in my mothers eyes, she did not look very happy.

My Father had just left the house, to his wee job down at the Canon's Hall at St Machan's, with a big smile on his face, and a few quid in his pocket from yours truly.

My mother said, 'Thomas, your dad cannae go to Canada.'

'Whit dae you mean he cannae go?'

It was then that I knew.

'Whit's up ma?' I said.

'Your Da has got Cancer, he has to go back to the hospital for treatment and he can't travel.

'When did you find this oot?'

'Just yesterday son, your father doesn't know, so keep it quiet.'

I was devastated. When you get told someone has got Cancer, it's very hard to take. But when it's your dad, man it's some weird feeling. A great friend of mine 'James Carr' who died in November 1975 also had Cancer. He was only twenty one. If I could have got my hands on God at that time, I would have choked him. James is sadly missed.

Thinking about my Da, I got angry. My Da never missed Mass once in his life, and never had a day off work through sickness. I would have given every penny of that money away to make him better, but sadly, it disnae work that way. When you think about it, money, it's nae good to you if you haven't any health to enjoy it. That's when I decided I was going to spend the lot, but slowly.

I remember about two weeks after I won the money; some wise person had put a letter into the Kirkintilloch Herald, saying what a terrible waste of money gambling was, and that I was a bad influence on young people. Well phuck them. I don't tell people how to spend their money, so nobody will tell me.

Anyway, back to the race. But before that I must digress again. I remember my first introduction to gambling. At 10 years of age I used to run to the bookies for my Aunt Margaret Connacher, every other day. With her three thrupenny doubles, and a tanner (sixpence) treble, she used to win quite often and she would reward me with a penny or two. That's when I realised that there was money to be made at the gee-gees. Little did I know. But over the years I've been lucky.

Way back then, when there was 240 pennies in the pound, a pound seemed like a lot of money. Now there is one hundred. But look out, just round the bend is the Euro-dollar. Its coming, and there's nothing gonnae stoap it.

A couple of years ago I walked into the bookmakers at about 11am. I looked up at the screen and right before my very eyes was live racing from Bluffontein, South Africa. Well I was stunned. Whit nixt? I can just see it all in the future. We will have the

'Cosmic Stakes', the 'Cosmic Dollar', the 'Alpha Centauri Stakes', the 'Sirius Derby'. I'm tellin' yees, it's comin' you can joost imagine it, in about fifty years time, yir sittin in the Bowling Club some night and Tommy Cairney's Grandson, the bingo caller, says, 'And now ladies and gentlemen, it's eyes down for the Andromeda Galaxy Snow-ball'. It's comin', for sure.

Well it's back to the race in hand, 'The Grand Theft Sperm Stakes.' What the hell do women really want eh? It disnae matter what you give them, they still want more. If you have got ten thousand pounds, they want eleven, you cannae win. So here comes the third furlong, hold on tae yir horses.

Hughie Differ, a friend of mine, and a fellow horse-player, was renowned for having long lie-ins in bed, especially at the weekends.

His mother shouted, up the stairs, 'Hugh its ten to eleven!'

And Hughie gave the instant gamblers retort, 'Gees a shout when it's even money.'

ENCOUNTER

As I came over Campsie glen very early one morning, I spotted a strange light landing down in the Clachan. As I approached the strange craft, two men alighted from the vehicle. I introduced myself, and they told me they had come from a distant galaxy.

They asked where they had landed, and I said, "this is Scotland."

Then one of them asked me if he could take a photograph of me next to their spaceship, for their photo album.

I said, "nae bother!"

So I asked if I could photograph them. They refused and said that they were working casual, and did not want to be shopped.

I said, "Och, ye'll no get shopped in Campsie."

"Campsie, that name rings a bell." Said one of the aliens.

Then they told me that once they were in this pub on a distant planet many light years away. They met three Scottish guys. They said that one was from Campsie and the other two were skint as well.

T.C.

The Lanarkshire Charity XI that played at the weekend. Back row (l. to r.)—Phil McAuley (Plymouth), Harry Haddock (Clyde), Jim McAuley (Dunfermline), Pat McLaughlin (Celtic), Jim Kennedy (Dunfermline), John Baxter (Hibernian).

Front—Chic Cairney (Celtic), Gerry Mays (Kilmarnock), Bobby Carroll (Celtic), Joe Reilly (Albion Rovers), and Billy Malone (Kilmarnock).

THIRD FURLONG

August 9th – September9th

Yvonne said to me one Sunday night, 'Tam, you will have to come in to Rottenrow Hospital tomorrow. My mum can't make it.' I said, 'No way. What do you need me for? You are only getting a photo of your belly, for gods sake, there's nothing I can do.' But that was not good enough.

Her plans were not working out, and she did not like it. She was trying to draw me deeper into the web of deceit that she had created. And now the going was getting heavy, very heavy indeed So we fell out again as that feeling of being took for granted refused to leave me. I felt like running away, but nah, I'm too old for all that. Or was I? I was so mixed up. Take me drunk, I'm hame.

Well why should I? It was not me who wanted to bring a child into this world, it was her. So she could bring up the wean.

So she went into the hospital in Glasgow for the scan on the Monday morning and obviously I was concerned about her. Well, I did not hear a word from her that day, or the following day but on the Wednesday afternoon, I got another wee note through my door. It read:

Tam

Could you give me

back my Bryan Adams tape

Yvonne.

Not a mention of the scan. 'So,' I thought, 'the little vixen is still trying to draw the old dog fox into the web of deception.' I was not taking the bait but I decided to put a note through her door. It said:

Yvonne

Could you please give me

back my sperm.

T.C.

Obviously she would not like it, too bad. I was fed up with her playing 'Postman Pat' so I told her to leave me alone for a wee while. Maybe I would come round to her way of thinking, but, I doubted it. Stoap the race! I have been free and single all my days, and I'm damn sure a twenty-seven year old novice, is gonnae change me at this stage of the human race.

There's a song out just now, called 'I Believe I Can Fly', It's great. Well ever since I had a bad accident in June1987. When I fell 18 feet from a faulty scaffold, I get the same dream that I can fly. It's brilliant that dream, but like most dreams, they never come true, and so I find myself once again, sitting at the 17th tee. My mind floating backwards, to, the days when I used to 'shoot the craw', or 'head South' with my mates.

I remember one time I came home from England, and my mother said to me. 'Thomas, is there any washin' machines doon in England'. Every time I arrived back home, my suitcase was full of dirty laundry.

I remember a few times, when we caught the 'Midnight Choo-Choo to Alabam', or the 23.50 to Bristol. Eventually we would arrive in Torquay. The one that sticks out the most was Colin 'Swifty' Smith and I were 'Shootin the Craw' again. It was a Friday night when we landed at Glasgow Central Station, and I mean, landed. Late as usual, and both of us full of the joys of spring, and the Famous Grouse.

We had just bought the tickets, at exactly 23.45. As we were running for the train we spotted one of those electric buggies that pull the mail, suitcases, etc. Swifty shouted to the driver 'Can you gees a lift pal, platform 14'. And before the guy could answer, Swifty was sitting next to him, pouring a Grouse into a plastic cup. Shouting, 'Avante! Avante!

So there we were on a wee train, heading for the Midnight Choo-Choo, to Ciderland. We shook hands with the driver, and said cheerio. Swifty was still shaking the guy's hand, when I turned and shouted, 'Come on you, hurry up sir'. Then they were cuddling each other.

Eventually when the train started to pull out, I said to Colin.

'Did you know that guy?'

'Aye' he said, 'That guy used to be a Professor at University. His marriage broke up because of his drink problem'.

Cest la vie, cheers.

Another amigo of mine John 'Paul Belmondo' Young, who probably got the Midnight Choo-Choo more times than anybody, told me that he knew every porter and ticket collector, by their first names, on the West Coast line.

So, as I stare up to the Finn Glen, I can see 'Megs Hole', filling up with the grey clouds. The rain is about five minutes away so I better head on home for the home made soup. But before I go, my eyes look towards the graveyard, where I can almost see my Grannies, and Grandfather Craven's gravestone. My Grannies sister was Lizzie McIvor, who lived down Rowantree 'Tar-row' where I was born. I remember it so vividly, and I can taste the home made lentil soup, with the big lumps of ham. I can actually taste it just now as I am writing this.

Whenever you went into Lizzie's, or my Grannie's, you could guarantee that the big pot of soup would be simmering away. And there was no way you left that house without being well fed. Smashing people, how I miss those 'hungry' years.

Well that must be three o' clock, the school bell has just rung, and here comes the rain. Just in time to soak the weans. Well I'll mosey down the road. The old muscles are stiffening up. Just think, I might have a child going to school at St. Machan's. Or will I? Stoap the race!

Thinking about the dinner, I suddenly remember an old joke about the two cannibals sitting down to a large meal. One of the cannibals says, 'See my wife, I cannae stand her.'

His pal says, 'Well shut up, and joost eat the chips'.

As I opened my door and looked down, there was another note from Yvonne, saying that she wanted to see me, and call a truce. I

Mother and Father 20th September 1946

joost threw it in the bin. Wummin eh! They just don't listen, do they? As I was sitting in the scullery waiting on the dinner, my mind started drifting again.

I was thinking about Mickey Rooney, the actor. He got married eight times. He must have been a masochist, or just damn crazy. I know guys and wummin that are married, and they hate it. What is the point of living with someone when you are not happy? Or maybe I am missing something, or have been lucky. But I've been assured by many people that I'm better off the way I am.

It's all that arguing and bickering that I could not put up with. But, there was soon to be a wee foal of mine entering this world, and I was responsible for it. No matter which way I studied the form, I was the sire and that was that.

And so the third furlong was coming to and end and the going was considerably heavier, but the race must go on. And then suddenly, I could hear the black beer calling me from the Commancero. I must go, it's a far, far, greater need, for a man must have his beer. So hold on to your ponies boys, were moving into the fourth furlong. Take me drunk, I'm hame.

Many years ago, Jeremy Thorpe, the Liberal M.P, appeared on the Michael Parkinson show. Near the end of the show, Parky said to Jeremy, 'Is there any great personal ambition, that you have never fulfilled?'

'Oh yes', said Jeremy.

'And what was that?'

'I would love to have ridden the winner of the Derby.'

'Oh you mean 'Troy?' said Parky.

'Oh no,' said Jeremy, 'Willie Carson!'

Lennox Amateurs F.C. - 1971

The Lennox Amateur side who lost 5-4. Back row (l. to r.)—Smith, G. Kincaid, P. Kincaid, Ginlay, J. Smith, Rae, McKenna. Front—Campbell, Carr, Craven, Rugvie and Cassidy.

FOURTH FURLONG

Approximately September 10th – October 10th

One afternoon I was sitting in the Commancero with Texas Jim having a couple of black beers. Jim says, 'Well I think it's theft Tam, theft by deception.'

'I think yir right Jim. I've been treated like a sperm bank', says I.

'Well, if I was you I'd go to the polis, you've been robbed'. Said Texas, 'Maybe you should get a Q.C'.

'Aye, aboot two bottles of Q.C. Well I'm off Jim, doon the road. See you later, are you not going home, or are you going the distance?' The Commancero was Jim's second home.

'I'm going the distance Tam, I'm an out and out stayer, is that you away fur yir oats?'

'Very funny Jim, see you later'.

As I passed Yvonne's flat, there was a light on. I was tempted to knock on the door but I didn't. Sometimes it's better to be left alone. Time seems to mend people's differences and anyway, I was in no mood for any tongue fencing.

Sometimes I try to look into the future, say, about six months time, when the baby will be born. What am I gonnae do, how am I gonnae react? I just don't know. Will it be a boy, or a girl? Who cares, as long as it's healthy.

Och, my mind is in a daze, wummin eh, they would drive you bananas. Especially during the summer when you see them walking doon the street half naked. Absolute magic!

You joost cannae help yirsel' lookin'. When I am walking past a good lookin' woman, I always say hello. Then I wait about four or five yards, then I turn round. I cannae help it, its natural isn't it. But sometimes you get caught. She turns roon at the same time as you. Ah! But whit's she doing eh? She's looking at your bum. That's a racing certainty, believe me.

Since I was about fifteen years of age, I have bumped into about three hundred and twenty seven lamp posts, honest. I've burst my face so many times, that nae wummin will look at me noo, they just look at my bum.

Can you imagine getting charged with looking at somebodys bum eh? You're sitting in the court and the judge says, 'You are charged with staring at Mrs Smiths posterior. Have you anything to say?'

'Aye, Mi Lord, bloody marvellous.'

This old lady phoned up the polis one day and said, 'There's a streaker who runs past my house every morning at half past six.'

The polis say, 'Don't you worry Mrs Smith, we'll get it stoaped immediately.'

'Och son, I don't want it stopped, I just want him to slow doon a wee bit.'

And so it was off to bed with the Sandman, hoping for the flying dream once again. The brain eh! It's a fascinating organ. Every time I think about it, I truly believe that there is a God out there. But sometimes I truly have my doubts, like a lot of people.

I remember a priest says to me years ago, 'Tom, I've not seen you at mass for a wee while.' I thought for a wee second and said, 'Father, the reason I was not there is, because I was somewhere else.' I walked away. He could think what he liked. One of the biggest problems I remember about being brought up a Catholic was the way it was drummed into you. I did not like it. And when old Canon McCabe used to go on his rounds, pontificating, almost everybody used to be terrified, kidding on they were not in . Shittin' themselves from the big man in the black cape.

Religion is a fear that's been instilled in man for centuries. It doesn't matter what or who your God is, there is good and bad everywhere. I don't like people who seem to think that they are above you. Whether it be priests, ministers, MPs etc. My parents always taught me that there was nobody better than me, and that I was no better than anybody else. No matter their position in life, colour or creed or profession. None above, none below. I personally think that children should be taught astronomy, from a very early age. So that they can understand how insignificant mankind is to the overall size of the cosmos.

Because it seems to me that the grown up people of this world do not. There is a giant star called 'Betelgeux', which is 150 million miles in diameter, one if billions. Now if that does not make you feel small, what will?

Talking about brains, I knew a guy called John McMahon, 'Macky' from Milton of Campsie, who was very intelligent and his patter was magic. John was one of the best football players in the district and should have reached higher financial fields than he did. He was not the only one but the guy was too laid back. He was too fond of La Dolce Vita, and who could blame him for loving the horses, the beer, and the women. A lot like some of the present day players, who have been lucky enough to have made the grade. Macky was once a guest of Her Majesty, in a big iron boarding house called Barlinnie.

In order to get an easier time in jail, Macky pretended to be mentally unstable. So one day he had an appointment with the prison psychiatrist. The doctor was holding a yellow snooker ball in his hand, and said to Macky, 'John, I want you to imagine this is an orange, and I want you to eat it.'

Well the poor doctor did not know who he was dealing with. Macky answered, 'OK doctor, you peel it first, then Ill eat it.'

Early one morning Macky was sitting at the Milton Cross, lapping up the sunshine and the chilled lager. An elderly gentleman, who was going to his work, shouted to Macky, 'Lovely morning, John.'

Macky replied instantly, 'Sure is Willie, it's one of those kind of mornings, if I had been working, I would have taken the day aff.'

There was no answer to that statement.

A friend of mine, Andrew Murray, told me he came home one time, after a hard day at the bookies and said to his father, Old Jimmy, 'How did your horses go the day, Da?'

Jimmy who was always very dramatic, put his hand in the air, and said, 'You wouldnae believe it son, three hoarses let me doon, for a right good treble.'

Amen.

James Argue of St Johnstone does the business against Tommy McClean of Rangers

THE FIFTH FURLONG

Approximately October 11th - November 10th

And so we were moving into the fifth furlong and Yvonne and I were talking again. She had brought two books with her, to pick the weans name.

'Joost call it Jake or Jenny,' I said. 'I quite like those names.'

'No way,' She said. 'I don't like those names.'

'Well suit yirsel', I don't really care what its name is, as long as he's alright.'

'What do you mean, he?' She said.

'Cos it's gonnae be a boy, and I will be calling him Jake, OK. You can call him whatever you like. As far as I am concerned, his name will be Jake, and that's that.'

And so we fell out again. Us guys joost cannae win. Stoap the race! It's nae wonder some guys want to strangle their wives. I remember a wee story in the Daily Mirror. I read it way back in the seventies. This is true. This guy who lived in Warsaw, Poland, twenty stories up in the high rise flats. His wife had left him and he could not stand the torment of living without her anymore. He decided to jump. But as he jumped, he did not know that his wife had decided to return to him. Believe it or not, he landed on top of her, and killed her, but he survived. The poor bastard. Noo, that's the type of guy who should not bet on horses. He had absolutely nae luck at all.

Then, there was this other poor man whose wife had left him. He couldn't stand the pain any more. So he was just about to put his head in the oven, when he heard a knock on the door.

'She's back, she's back!', he thought. He opened the door and there was a strange man standing.

'Whit dae you want?' He shouted angrily.

'I've come from Littlewoods.' said the stranger.

'What! How much have I won?' he smiled expectantly.

'Nothin,' said the man, 'I've joost came to tell you, yir wife has been arrested fur shoplifting.'

Nae luck at aw. Stoap the race!

Life, eh? It's joost the same as gambling, you need the luck. Without it you have no chance. And so I find myself once more, sitting on the wee hummock at the 17th tee. It's a beautiful day as I stare out away over the Dumbarton Hills, reminiscing back to the time when I was in Jersey, in the Channel Islands, 1969.

I landed in St Helier along with two mates, Ian Young and Hugh O'Hare. Anyway to cut a long story short, I had got a job for a week, and Hughie got some casual at the docks. Youngie made oor pieces on cheese up. After three weeks we were destitute, and desperate, so Ian and I decided to come home. We managed to scrape up the boat fare to Weymouth. We landed there about three o clock in the afternoon, skint and absolutely ravenous. We went to the Social Security. They gave us ten shillings each (fifty pence).

Then after fish and chips, we were sitting down at the beach, staring out to sea. It was starting to get dark. I said to Ian, 'Well Ian its five hundred miles north to Campsie. Lets go.'

We started walking. As we got to the outskirts of Weymouth, the rain came on. Nae luck. I felt like throwing my suitcase into a field, but we struggled on. After about an hour, an old Ford Anglia stopped. The driver asked us where we were going.

'Eh, Scotland, Glasgow.' We said.

He laughed, 'Glasgow' he said, 'Jump in, I will drop yous off at a transport café four miles up the road.'

Brilliant, at least we were out of the rain.

The café had just closed. Nae luck. But the lady gave us a cup of tea through the window. After we had explained our predicament, she directed us to a place called Batcombe Friary. 'Just along the road', she said. About four Irish miles it turned out. We arrived at the Friary, totally shattered. We knocked on a huge door, and a huge friar appeared. He must have been about seven foot twelve. Nae problem, they put us up for the night in the dormitory.

Next morning they gave us breakfast of lumpy porridge, toast and tea. It was lovely. When you are starving you will eat almost anything. Then they gave us a lift up to Yeovil, God Bless them. When something like that happens to you, it restores your faith in mankind, and makes you a better person.

Anyway, we eventually got to the outskirts of London. Ian had decided to go to Maidstone in Kent, where his mate Alec Coll was living. I decided to go home so we divided the money up, which was very little. Ian headed east, and I took the high road.

It was about thirty-six hours later, I was standing in Springburn waiting on the Campsie bus. The bus arrived and I told the conductor, who was Frank Hardy from Twechar, that I had no money. He said, 'Just go upstairs and I'll take your name and address.' Luckily for me, Jim Argue was there. Jim was just back from a training session at Perth. He was playing for St. Johnstone and was a regular in the first team. Jim paid my bus fare, and also gave me a few bob. That's something I've never forgotten. James Argue was one of the nicest guys I've ever met and I can honestly say that I've never heard a bad word said about him. Another true gentleman who is sadly missed.

Anyway the race must go on. We were heading for the sixth furlong, coming into the straight. The going was getting a bit easier, as I was beginning to accept the fact that I was gonnae be a father. Somebody had told me that I did not know how lucky I was. There's probably thousands of guys who would love to be in the same position.

As I said before, I did not plan it, she did. The human race cannot be stopped. So 'Postman Pat', had dropped another wee note through my door. Yvonne wanted another truce. 'OK', I said. She had brought me a few black beers, and we sat and had a wee blether.

After a while she says to me, 'Tam, will you marry me?'

I said, 'Certainly, who to?'

'Very funny Tam.' she says.

I said, 'I will marry you on the condition we get divorced the next day.'

I joost don't believe I could get married. Merry – aye! And so, Yvonne went away in the huff again. Wummin eh! They'd drive you up the wall. Then suddenly I heard the black beer calling me from the Commancero.

I had to go. As I left the house, I said to the picture of St. Teresa. I'm joost goin' for a couple of black beers. Keep yir eye in the house fur me. I really am glad, and looking forward to being a dad, but don't tell Yvonne that. OK Teresa, I'll not be long.

I was sittin' at the bar with Texas Jim. He just told me he'd had a hard day at the racing, trying to pick winners but had come out winning in the end. Jim said, 'There's too many races Tam. Every ten minutes. The bookies have got it sown up, yiv hardly time tae lift yir drink.'

'Aye, yiv got a hard time of it Jim.' Said I.

'I feel sorry for wee Johnny, (Johnny, was the punters runner to the bookies across the street), running up and doon tae 'Raymond Chandlers' every two minutes. He's goin' through three pairs of wellies a week, it's just not fair on him.'

'Ach, well Jim, he seems happy enough, and he gets a few bob for it.'

And so after a few black beers, Texas Jim told me about a young lady he was engaged to about twenty-five years ago. Jim played guitar in a rock and roll band, and he said it was murder because he was plagued by groupies. His fiancée had broken off their engagement because of all his late nights, and the girls chasing him. But Jim says that was not the real reason for the split.

'What was the reason Jim?' I asked.

'It was because I was faking orgasms.'

Well I was still laughing twenty minutes later when I was going to bed. What a man. Now we were moving into the sixth furlong. Into the dark months ahead. Hold on to yir horses boys and girls, there's still a good bit to go.

SIXTH FURLONG

Approximately 11th November - 12th December

Now we were more than half way through this human race and Yvonne was beginning to feel the pace. Now and then she would be moaning to me, about this and that, and being pregnant.

'Well, I said. You wanted to get pregnant, so stoap yir moaning to me. I'm fed up listening to you. My mother had six weans and she never moaned the way you are. I remember when I was born, the next day my mother was back at her work, doon the pit at Kilsyth, doing a twelve hour shift, so joost stoap yir complaining to me.'

'Yir mother did not work down the pit.' Yvonne said.

'Oh yes she did. Aye, six days a week, twelve hours shifts. And brought up six weans.'

'I don't believe you Tam.'

'It's the truth, honest.'

I was getting more like wee Angus Darroch every day. Obviously I was kidding her but if it made her stop moaning for a while, it was worth it.

It's the same when you see horse trainers, jockeys etc. getting interviewed on the telly. You know they are lying through their teeth, and they know that you know. Do you think that they are gonnae tell Joe Public when a certain horse is gonnae win? No way, and who can blame them? I certainly would not.

But, talking about moaning, some people just never stoap. Moan, moan, moan. They complain about the weather, the time, the prices in the shops, anything. People just like to moan. But the weather, what is the point, there's nothing we can do about it. It would drive you crazee mental. Why don't people laugh a bit more, and be kinder to their neighbours? After all, we are only here for a wee while anyway. Life is really weird, as soon as we are born we are on the road to death. So it's better to stoap yir moaning and have a good laugh. I remember years ago when my ma and da used to take the family on holiday to places like Saltcoats and Portobello, Ardrossan and Ayr.

They were the days eh! Place like Largs, and Troon, you actually thought that they were on the other side of the world. But noo, folk are goin' tae Paris and Rome for the weekend. I mean, who could have though that horse trainers would be sending horses to the other side of the world to race.

I can joost imagine in about fifty years time, people will be flying to the Moon and Mars for the week-end, honest, its coming. Mind you, some people don't have to go, they are already there anyway. Just picture this:

'Hi Tam, how you doing, where are ye goin the night?'

'Och I'm joost nippin' over to Bueno Aries fur a pint, Willie.'

'Oh great Tam, can ye dae me a favour?'

'Aye sure Willie, whit is it?'

Bring us back a fish supper, will ye?'

'Aye, nae bother Willie.'

I'm tellin' yis, it's comin'. That's progress, and there's nothin' we can do about it. I was sitting in wee Angus Darrochs (The sage of Slatefield) house one day having a dram or two. Jimmy Allen, Cormack Finlay and I listened as Angus poured out the drinks. The more drinks that were poured, the more the lies were told. One minute you were at the North Pole, then you were in the Australian Outback, then deepest Africa. Angus had been everywhere. Every now and then Jimmy would say to Angus.

'Och yir phuckin arse Angy, ye don't know wan end of a boat from anither. Ye got the train in tae Queen Street Station wance, and ye thought Glesca wus covered.'

But Angus joost ignored Jimmy and got on with the fabrication.

One day I said to them, just to annoy them.

'What is the coldest country in the world?'

'Siberia.' Said Angus.

'Antartica.' Jimmy said.

‘No.’ I said.

‘North Pole.’ Said Angus.

‘No way.’

‘Iceland.’ Says Angus, getting fed up.

‘No.’

‘Well whit is it, we give in.’

‘Chile.’ Said I

‘Ya big swine ye,’ said Angy, angrily. Jimmy joost laughed.

‘Have you ever been to Tibet Angus?’ I said.

‘Tibet,’ Said Angus. ‘I know every street in Tibet, I wus a taxi driver there fur four years.’

Well you couldnae argue with the Sage of Slatefield.

Then Jimmy told us the story about a wee Irish horse trainer, who had brought one of his horses over to run in a big race at Ascot. The Irish trainer was down at the start feeding his horse some imperial mints, and the steward of the Jockey Club, the Duke of Norfolk, got wind of it.

The Duke arrived at the start, and said to the trainer, ‘I hope you are not giving that horse dope.’

‘Oh no, your worship, here, you eat some and I’ll eat some.’

So they both tasted a few mints. Two or three minutes later the wee Irish trainer said to the jockey, ‘Look Pat, just keep up with the pace to about a furlong out, then press the button. If you see anything passing you, don’t worry, it will either be me or the Duke of Norfolk.’

And so the sixth furlong was coming to a close and Yvonne and I had fell oot again. I was beginning to wonder if there was any point in going on with the relationship. Obviously the way I was deceived was never gonnae leave me. I just could not help that feeling. There’s an old saying ‘Forgive ‘n’ Forget’. Aye it’s easy to forgive, but I joost cannae forget. It’s really very difficult, but the race must go on, and I swear I can hear the black beer calling me from the Commancero. I swear Tom Grant has got some kind of invisible radar or something that attracts us to the black beer. Or maybe I'm joost fond of it. So I must go. Texas Jim will be there and you are guaranteed a laugh. What is life eh, without a few beers, a few winners, a good laugh, and a greetin' faced wummin?

Cheers.

THE SEVENTH FURLONG

Approximately 13th December - 13th January 1998

Indeed! 'Come into my parlour', said the spider to the fly. Well that's the way it happened. She had cast the invisible web of deceit all over me and I was entangled. There was no escape, no way out. Somebody call the Polis!

Us guys have no chance, I'm telling yis boys, get out while you can. You cannae win honest. Trust me, I've been there. It's the same with the horses, you cannot win. We are all living in delusions of grandeur. But the question must remain, what else is there, we were brought up with it, its part of our life, and its hard to change. I've been gonnae chuck the beer, the horses and the wummin fur years, but I cannae, gees a break big man, I hear you say. Take me drunk, I'm hame.

Once we've had a few black beers, whit happens eh? You have a wee punt, hopefully a few winners. Then you get randy, then you know what happens next. Doors start to get chapped when the sun goes down, and the libido goes up. Oh aye, the midnight ramblers go on the prowl. Even the female species, so watch out boys, they're out to get you.

And talking about horses, if you are gonnae have a bet, make it each way, especially each way if the horse is 4-1 or over. If it's placed, you will get your money back. A couple of pals of mine who bet on the horse had £20 to win on a horse at 12-1. I had £10 each way on the same horse. It came in second, I got £40 back, and they got nothing. Who's daft, eh? It's greed that beats most gamblers, all the time

But the race goes on and Yvonne is going to her maws for Xmas. As usual we fell out over the name of our future child, and other things. She had gone for another photograph at Rottenrow, but I had not seen it. Just before she left at the beginning of January to stay with her mum, she put the photo through my door. That's it on the back page. But later I was to find out that she had no intention of calling the wean Jake, or Jenny. See what I mean, devious, eh!

So Xmas and New Year came and went. Mine was very quiet. It just hasn't got the same appeal anymore. The New Year seems to be celebrated more in England than here, but obviously I prefer Scotland. I got a chance of a ticket for the Celtic v Rangers game at the New Year but I refused it. I'm absolutely fed up with all the bigotry, and jingoism that goes with it. And I mean on both sides. The sooner it is stamped out, the better. Wouldn't it be nice to see Celtic and Rangers fans intermingled at an Old Firm match? Or is that maybe asking too much? Maybe it would lose its appeal.

Big Paddy Malarkey, a Celtic supporter, died. So he's standing in the queue at the gates of heaven and St. Peter shouts, 'Next, name.'

'Paddy Malarkey.'

St. Peter pressed some buttons on his computer. 'I'm sorry, ye cannae get in. Yiv no got enough points.'

'How know, I've been a good punter, Your Worshipfullness, how can I get merr points?' said Paddy.

'You will have to go back down to Earth, and dae something virtually impossible, or you will be shovelling coal for the rest of time.' said Peter.

'Well, what do you want me to do.'

'You must go back down, and help Celtic win the league.'

'Och, joost gees the shovel.' said Paddy.

And so the seventh furlong is coming to an end and the bad weather is moving in. Yvonne is staying down at her mum's in Ayrshire to have the baby. And now its all uphill in the last two furlongs.

Maybe I won't see her again. Ach, but I know I will once the boy is born. It's due on the seventh of March. Beware the Ides of March. But later on I would be told that the child was born a week after the event. Stoap the race! Nice one eh?

THE EIGHTH FURLONG

Approximately 14th January - 15th February

Moving into the last 440 yards, the going was still a bit heavy. A friend of mine asked me how Yvonne and I were getting on.

'Magic, I've not seen her for about three weeks. We seem to get on better when we don't see each other.'

'Well, there's not much chance of yous falling out if yous don't see each other.' said the friend.

'Aye, very true.' I said.

Relationships eh! Who needs them? I would rather have a good book. I remember a book I once read called, 'The Zarkon Principle.' It was brilliant. This book reckoned that Jesus Christ disappeared for seventeen years. From thirteen years of age to thirty. It reckons there is no record where he went. The writer says that Jesus either went walkabouts, to places like India, Far East etc. to learn about different cults and medicines, or that he travelled in a spaceship back to wherever. Hence the seventeen years. Well wherever he went, I hope he is getting a few winners.

I think its about time he was back doon here, tae sort oot the mess that we're in. But it's really man that has created the chaos. All this nonsense about religion and God would drive you crazy. People should respect other people's beliefs, and try to remember that nobody knows who God is anyway. What a load of nonsense. Personally I think that greed and selfishness has a lot to do with the problem. People should try to be content with what they have got.

I remember one day I was sitting down at Castle Circus, in Torquay, along with an assortment of charlatans and blaggards. They came from all over Britain, from every nook and cranny. There was this Geordie lad who said to the company, 'I am not looking for much in this life, just a deaf and dumb nymphomaniac, that owns an off licence.'

Well who isn't.

ALBA CALEDONIA ECOSSE SCOTIA

People must go to places,
To brighten up
Their sad lonely faces.

People must return,
To the one who did make them.
Then be born again.

But I go to Scotia,
In my dreams every night,
To the land of my people.
It's such a terrible fight.

And some day I will get there,
To my own lovely glen,
So I must be strong,
As you never know when.

So I'll look down on Scotia
From a spiritual high.
They tell me I'm dying,
I'll never, ever say, goodbye.

Thomas Craven

Dedicated to the memory of my late Uncle Louis Convery, who told me that he would never return to Scotland.

And so its back to the race. I keep thinking, 'How am I gonnae react when this wean is born?' Everyday I think about it. It's driving me bananas. Ach, take me drunk, I'm hame.

Once again I find myself sitting up at the 17th tee. Staring up to Campsie Glen and up to the Blane Valley. I shake my head out of the reverie. Well, the wean will soon be entering into this world, and I was responsible, that's a fact, Jack. There is no point in looking at the past, it's gone. I must face up to the future, and bring the child up. I suppose it's the same with bigotry, why cant people forget the past, and get on with the future, it's crazy. Then I recall what Roberto Burns once said:

Pleasures are like poppies spread,
We seize the flower, it's bloom is spread,
Or like the snow, falling on the river,
One moment white, then gone forever.

What a man.

PLEASE SET ME FREE

"Please set me free, the dolphin cried,
Before it gets too late.
All the others stayed and died,
Please open the gate."

"Let me swim out to the sea,
Far from this lonely pen."
The dolphin cried, "Please set me free,
And let me smile again."

"I've loved and lost and loved once more,
Out there under the oceans.
Until I was captured and brought ashore,
They try to control my emotions".

"I do what they want, though I'm getting
weak,
But my mind is still strong.
If only they could hear the words I speak,
They'd know they're doing wrong.

"Please set me free", the dolphin cried,
"Let me be with the ones I love".
With words unheard, the night he died,
And swam to the sea above.

John Robertson

THE FINAL FURLONG.

16th February - 10th March.

And so this human race is coming to an end. Yvonne was given the 7th of March for the baby's arrival. She is still down in Ayrshire at her mums. And I must admit I am looking forward to it. But, for obvious reasons, we have not been in touch. That old feeling of emotional blackmail is never gonnae leave me, but I must live with it. I cannot help the way I feel. But who can, what's done is done, so lets get on with it. There is no doubt that I cannae win the race. But maybe the second prize will be the greatest consolation. I will get my sperm back in the shape of a wee baby.

And so it was on the tenth of March I received a letter with no stamp, stating that, Matthew Austin Geddes, had been born on the third of March 1998, weighing in at 7lbs 6ozs. I was flabber-gasted. It took a week to let me know. The half of Scotland knew about it before I did. Why did they make me wait a week to let me know? Well, I guess, she was just running true to form.

To say I was angry was an understatement, so I decided I had to go and see my boy. The next morning I got dressed up to go, but I missed the bus. I thought, that must be an omen so I phoned to let her know I was coming down. While I was talking to Yvonne, I overheard her mother saying, 'Tell him to get lost.'

I said to Yvonne, 'I heard that.'

Her mother came on the phone and gave me dogs abuse.

I said, 'Did Yvonne tell you that she had planned to get pregnant and had told me a pack of lies. She said that she was on the pill.'

'So what?' She said.

'So what, do my feelings not count?' I said.

'We don't need you.' she said.

Well I hung up. There's no point in arguing with anybody on a phone. It seemed to me that there was something funny about her mother's answer. 'So what?' 'Very strange.

Then I went and bought some beer and went home disgusted. Ye

Look who's arrived!
Born on
and weighed

cannae win, no way. But I could not drink the beer. Drink never solved any problems.

And so once again I'm sitting at the 17th tee. What the hell is this life all about? Wummin, eh, wummin, you have no chance. I jeost cannot understand them. First I get deceived and robbed, then all of a sudden big daddy is public enemy number one. Take me drunk, I'm hame, whit's happening? Send fur Darroch.

Then, lo and behold, I got another letter. 'Please phone me Tam.' But not when her mother was in. Well I phoned, and have done two or three times. I asked her to come back, and maybe through time our relationship would develop. But it seems as though its got to be on her terms. She wants me to make a solid commitment. But I cannot guarantee that after what's happened, but I know eventually, everything will turn out fine in the end. And then later on when the wee barra can kick a ball, he'll always be with me. I'll be very proud to bring him up, and if Celtic or Rangers want to sign him, I don't care. There's no bias in my heart.

Then suddenly I can hear the black beer calling me once again from the Commancero. I must go, for a man needs his beer. This human race has finished and I have lost, but I have gained a son.

HASTA LA VISTA.

ABOVE: James Carr with May Fitch

LEFT: This is my father's cousin, Michael Craven, alongside Willie Wallace when they played for Kelvinside Thistle. Willie went on to play for Celtic, and to win the European Cup in 1967. Several people have told me that Mick was a better player than Willie, but it's always the same old story – you need the luck.

NIEVE

There won't be snow,
In the place where
I am going,
But there will be love,
In the seeds
That I've been sowing.

There won't be snow
On the hills
Where I'll be roaming.
But there will be hair
On the head
That I'll be combing.

There won't be snow,
In my heart,
Or in my soul,
For my snow must remain
In Espanol.

T.C.

UPDATE

8.30 am, Monday August 24th 1998

As I passed Yvonne's door I noticed that the roses I had left on her doorstep had been removed and her blinds were closed. I knew then that she was back.

As I thanked St. Teresa, I knocked on the door. She was looking well and I could hear Mathew in the background. Eventually when he was sitting on my knee, Yvonne shouted from the kitchen, 'Would you like tea or coffee?'

'Coffee.' I said, then Mathew whispered in my ear, 'It's good to be back dad.'

I couldn't believe it. I said, 'Welcome home son. It's good to see yous.'

THE BEGINNING.